T0381201

Did I Remember to Tell My Daughter?

Mother-Daughter Tips for Life

Dr. Sharon E. Peterson

AuthorHouse™
1663 Liberty Drive
Bloomington, IN 47403
www.authorhouse.com
Phone: 1 (800) 839-8640

© 2015 Dr. Sharon E. Peterson. All rights reserved.

No part of this book may be reproduced, stored in a retrieval system,
or transmitted by any means without the written permission of the author.

Published by AuthorHouse: 08/28/2015

ISBN: 978-1-5049-3227-1 (sc)
ISBN: 978-1-5049-3228-8 (e)

Library of Congress Control Number 2015914022

Print information available on the last page.

Any people depicted in stock imagery provided by Thinkstock are models,
and such images are being used for illustrative purposes only.
Certain stock imagery © Thinkstock.

This book is printed on acid-free paper.

This book is a work of non-fiction. Unless otherwise noted, the author and the publisher make no explicit guarantees as to the accuracy
of the information contained in this book and in some cases, names of people and places have been altered to protect their privacy.

Because of the dynamic nature of the Internet, any web addresses or links contained in this book may have changed
since publication and may no longer be valid. The views expressed in this work are solely those of the author and do not
necessarily reflect the views of the publisher, and the publisher hereby disclaims any responsibility for them.

KJV
Scripture quotations marked KJV are from the Holy Bible, King James Version (Authorized Version). First published in
1611. Quoted from the KJV Classic Reference Bible, Copyright © 1983 by The Zondervan Corporation.

ESV
Unless otherwise indicated, all scripture quotations are from The Holy Bible, English Standard Version® (ESV®). Copyright
©2001 by Crossway Bibles, a division of Good News Publishers. Used by permission. All rights reserved.

NLT
Scripture quotations marked NLT are taken from the Holy Bible, New Living Translation, copyright © 1996, 2004, 2007.
Used by permission of Tyndale House Publishers, Inc. Carol Stream, Illinois 60188. All rights reserved. Website

authorHOUSE®

Contents

FOREWORD

My most memorable impartations to the younger women have been to teach them the importance of prayer and fasting. I have been saved a very long time. I am now eighty-eight years old. I was baptized in Jesus Name and filled with the Holy Ghost coming up out of the water on June 15, 1961. In the fifty-four years of serving Jesus, God has given me much wisdom, knowledge, and understanding about life.

After I moved to Virginia from Queens, New York in 1980, I met my new daughter, Sharon Peterson at Zion Apostolic, Petersburg, Virginia. We both served with Bishop Dr. Samuel Wright, Sr. Pastor Peterson had a young son that my husband loved. I gave her instructions many times in her time of crisis. I imparted instruction with prayer and unconditional love. She was a single parent who needed guidance. I told her to fast and pray about everything. I imparted to her how to use the wisdom of God to manage her finances and keep the bill collectors from calling and knocking on the door. Keep a dollar and not spend your last. I gave her instruction about marriage and what it means to become one. I taught her many secrets to managing the home and caring for her family. It takes much patience in mentoring young women. In this hour, many of the younger women do not want to hear what the older women have to say. But thanks be to God, Sharon received many words of kindness, and wisdom to manage her life.

Helen Couch Hilliard

PREFACE

I desired to birth a little girl. But at my age it was too late. So I took into my home a beautiful little girl who was five years old. She was very precious and beautiful and full of life. She was born sickly with many challenges and challenges that would follow her for the next sixteen years of her life. She was a beautiful match for my home. Now she is in college, striving to achieve her goals in life. She has big dreams.

I wrote this book because I wanted to impart wisdom that can go with my daughter when she leaves home. In writing this book, I wanted to express my love and concerns for my daughter, Bria, and all young daughters who meet the challenges of everyday life. Many of them need someone to say to them, you can make the journey. These are words of wisdom that I desire to impart to all young daughters who are leaving the nest of their home. I want to encourage you not to be afraid of life, but be cautious. See life in its fullness through the eyes of God. If Jesus is not in your life, get to know him. Pay attention! You can learn from other people's mistakes without being judgmental.

As she is preparing to leave home, I asked myself, did I remember to tell my daughter?" I want to do everything in my power to prepare her for the future. This book is an impartation that will bless other mothers and their young women as well. I want the younger women to know, now is the time to get saved and live holy, love God with your whole heart. I could tell many stories about my journey with the Lord.

VALUE LIFE

You are a very special person! Know that God has given you this opportunity to live a full life in him. Jesus Christ is your Savior, and He loves every pound of you. He has designed you to be who you are. You are not a copy cat to anyone. Perhaps you favor your mother or dad, but you are different. He made one copy of you and moved on to the next design. You are fearfully and wonderfully made (Psalm 139:14) by the hand of God. After He created you, He assigned you to parents that raised you. They loved you and took care of you. They sacrificed much to care for you. This is your life and you must value every moment that you have in life. Take nothing for granted. Believe in Jesus! Believe in yourself and be encouraged to follow the Master's plan that He has for you. "For I know the thoughts that I think toward you, saith the LORD"

Jeremiah 29:11.

PERSONALITY

Show love to all. Wear a smile that is fixed in your skin. Be polite, brave, and compassionate. Show God's strength in your life to others.

My precious daughter, become a well rounded person. For the life you will lead, others will draw close to you because you represent Christ alone. Work hard at not being selfish. Learn to love unconditionally. It may be hard at first but with Christ you can do all things. He will strengthen you. Remember this scripture: **"I can do all things through Christ** who strengthens me" (Philippians 4:13).

Know yourself and live to Christ's expectations. Remember you will never please your flesh, neither will you please others.

Learn to enjoy life to the fullest in Christ, for there is an abundance of joy and peace in Christ that you have yet to experience.

OVERCOMING FEAR

There are different types of fear: danger fear and godly fear. According to Merriam dictionary, fear is an unpleasant often strong emotion caused by an anticipation or awareness of danger. Godly fear is a profound reverence and awe especially toward God. It is very natural to show fear or have fear. Just remember who you are. You are a prayer warrior. God has not given you the spirit of fear but of love, power, and a sound mind.

ON DRIVING

Practice driving and using skill as long as you want to drive. Ask Jesus to dispatch his angels around your vehicle and along the highway. Follow the rules. Do not follow another vehicle too closely. Always take your time; there is no need to rush. You will still reach your destination alive. Do not fumble looking for items in your car. Leaning to the floor is certainly against the rules.

Your vision will be twisted with your body and it will cause you to crash.

Do not speed! You will arrive safely and on time. If you want to arrive on time, leave on time. However, if you are already late, still take your time. You will have a good driving record and low rates with your insurance company.

ON DOING LAUNDRY

Always use cold water. Don't mix any colors with your white cloths. Wash sweaters separately. You can wash your dark towels with your jeans, but never mix sweaters and towels unless you want nap on your sweaters. Wash your pretty dresses separately on delicate. Follow the use of detergent in machine. You do not need to see bubbles to know your detergent is working. Washing at night is better on your light bill. Wash stockings by hand and hang in the bathroom. Do not put stockings in the dryer because the heat will diminish the wear and tear of stockings.

ON COOKING

Work at becoming an excellent cook. Start with being clean. Wash your hands often. Keep counter spaces clean and fresh. When food is on the stove, do not leave food unattended. Start on time to prepare food. Follow the directions of the recipes and your dish should come out just fine.

ON BANKING

Do not spend what you do not have. Keep a record of what you are spending and the bills you must pay each month on a ledger. Do not write checks if there is no money in the bank. Try to pay all your bills at the same time of the month. Don't get behind with payments on rent, mortgage, or car payment. Always keep extra money for emergencies. Save something every pay day for a rainy day. Some will tell you, pay yourself first, but I say give God his tithes first and then pay yourself.

"For I tell you, unless your righteousness exceeds that of Scribes and Pharisees, you will never enter the kingdom of heaven." (Matthew 5:20)

BUILD GOOD CREDIT

Build good credit. If you are not going to pay cash for items, then you need good credit. Get advice from your bank on how to start good credit. The bank can help you get established. If you get a credit card from the bank, use wisdom on how to charge on your account. You should be willing to pay back what you have spent within thirty days. If you cannot pay back in thirty days, don't charge. When you use your card, only charge what you can pay back by the time your bill comes in.

INVESTMENTS

Make investments early in life and allow your investments to grow. Do not withdraw your investments until you are ready to retire. Use wisdom in who to invest with and where you invest. Do not be afraid to get counsel from a reliable source. Do your homework. The following are web sites that would be excellent for you to look at: http://www.bankrate.com/finance/investing/how-to-become-a-millionaire-in-7-easy-hah-steps-1.aspx

http://moneyasyougrow.org/

Be a role model and leader in having your own home, buying a car with cash, living within your means and making sound investments (Ebony Magazine: Raising a Millionaire, page 95, July 2014). I highly recommend that you travel before marriage. Become a well rounded person.

ON GIVING

Be a giver and be glad. Pay your tithes and offering, and always have a seed to sow into the kingdom of God and you will reap the benefits. Learn how to sow with intelligence into other people's lives. Meaning, do not be unwise and sow into bad soil. Pick out a foundation and give to it. St. Jude Children's hospital is always a good choice. Give and the Lord will give back to you, pressed down and shaken together. God promised that he would "open the windows of heaven and pour you out a blessing that you will not have room to receive" (Malachi 3:8).

 Be a happy giver. Do not let anyone talk you out of paying your tithes. Jesus did not come to abolish what was written, but to fulfill it.

Matthew 5:17-20 ESV

"Do n ot think that I have come to abolish the Law or the Prophets; I have not come to abolish them but to fulfill them. For truly, I say to you, until heaven and earth pass away, not an iota, not a dot, will pass from the Law until all is accomplished. Therefore whoever relaxes one of the least of these commandments and teaches others to do the same will be called least in the kingdom of heaven, but whoever does them and teaches them will be called great in the kingdom of heaven. For I tell you, unless your righteousness exceeds that of the scribes and Pharisees, you will never enter the kingdom of heaven."

ON SHOPPING

Learn to be a wise shopper. Shop for what you need first. Put space in between the item that you want. Watch for item reduction. If it goes on sale, buy it. Buy cloths that will fit you and look good on you. Shop when you have money to spend in cash or when you have money in the bank. This way you will not be tempted to charge on the credit card. Do not allow your friends to use your bank card and pin numbers. Encourage friends to open their own bank account.

SHOPPING FOR FOOD

Always shop for plenty of fresh vegetables and fruits instead of can, frozen, or packaged goods. These goods are loaded with more sodium and are high in colesterol. Learn to read labels of food items. It will guide you in what to buy. Stay away from high sugary drinks. Train your apetite to eat at home instead of fast food. Pack a lunch for work. Stay away from lunch meats which are high in sodium and high in colesterol. Eat lots of fresh leafy green vegetables.

ON TECHNOLOGY

Do not allow technology to control your every move. Give it a rest. Do not sleep and eat technology. Take a break from it throughout the day. Do not sleep with your phone in your chest. It may cause cancer. Do your research. Be a teacher and train your mother how to use technology.

COLLEGE/UNIVERSITY/ TECHNICAL TRAINING SCHOOLS

You must plan for college. Try not to get into huge debt. Scholarships and government grants are available for those who did well academically in high school. If you did not do well in high school, attend a junior college. Stay focus on your goals and dreams. You must choose the career that you want to pursue. It is not mom or dad's choice to choose your career. It is which career you want to pursue in life. Be vigilant! Be determined to succeed in the career you chose. Make sure you choose a field that you can earn good money and be successful. Do not leave God out.

HOMEWORK

Put yourself on a schedule to do homework. In elementary and middle school, study at the kitchen or dining room table. In high school, or college, it's okay to study in private as long as the work is being done. Do not wait until the last minute. Use your time wisely. In college some classes are virtually conducted. Complete assignments as instructed and finish on schedule. If you need help, sign up for a tutor.

STUDY TO BE QUIET

You do not need to say something all the time about everything. You just don't belong in every conversation. The Word of God says in I Thessalonians 4:11 (KJV), "And that ye study to be quiet, and to do your own business, and to work with your own hands, as we commanded you".

In the NLT, "Make it your goal to live a quiet life, minding your own business and working with your hands, just as we instructed you before".

DREAM BIG

It is your dream, why not dream big. Dream big! Just make sure your dreams line up with God. You can accomplish incredible things in life if you align yourself with the Word of God. Just remember what God has said about you according to Jeremiah 29:11 (KJV), "For I know the plans I have for you, declares the LORD, plans to prosper you and not to harm you, plans to give you hope and a future".

SLEEPING LATE

Early birds catch the worms. Ants are hard workers. Train yourself to get up early and meet the Lord. Plan to go to work on time. Do not subject yourself to being lazy. You will feel better and have energy to complete your daily activities with grace.

MEET THE LORD EARLY

Make meeting the Lord early in the morning through prayer and reading God's Word and daily routine.

 (A Psalm of David when he was in the wilderness of Judah.) "O God, thou *art* my God; early will I seek thee: my soul thirsteth for thee, my flesh longeth for thee in a dry and thirsty land, where no water is" (*Psalms 63:1*).

 Psalms 5:3: "In the morning, O LORD, you hear my voice; in the morning I lay my requests before you and wait in expectation."

Psalms 55:17 17 "Evening, morning and noon I cry out in distress, and he hears my voice".

DOCTOR VISITS

Be on time for doctor visits. Keep a calendar of all visits. Stay on top of your health. Eat healthy and you will have less doctor visits. Eat a lot of the green stuff. Get plenty of consistent exercise and good sleep.

A good remedy for a cold virus is to drink plenty of water, and eat hot chicken soup. Drink hot water with lemon and honey to break up congestion. Get plenty of rest. Be consistent. The cold should clear up in a few days. However, be concerned if you have a fever. See a doctor!

FRIENDSHIPS

Make your friendships few. Keep true friendships solid. Be transparent in all relationships. Be who you are and love yourself and love your neighbors. If you do not have any friends, the Bible teaches that we should show ourselves friendly (Proverbs 18:24).

24"A man that hath friends must shew himself friendly: and there is a friend that sticketh closer than a brother".

Do not use your body to win friends. Do not use money or gifts to buy friendships. Use your intelligence to improve relationships. There will be many relationships that are not designed for you.

When you and your friends fall out; learn to forgive quickly. Move on with your life. Take each situation as a lesson learned. Avoid peer pressure. Be your own person and follow the teachings and wisdom of God.

GOOD WORK ETHICS

Working is a part of life. Even most handicap persons can work.
You have no excuse. Go to work and take good care of yourself.
Mom and Dad will not be with you always. When you get your
job, work on that job until you establish yourself. Do not change
jobs too frequently. Changing jobs too frequently can work against
your credit report.

PROCRASTINATION

If you are assigned to do something, do not drag your feet. Get it done! Do a good job. If you need help, ask for help. If you can't do it, why would you accept the assignment? If you do not want to do it, let someone else do the assignment. Make sure you stay in your lane.

RESPECT FOR ELDERLY

The elderly have much wisdom to impart to you. Most are genuinely concerned for your future life. Be willing to hear them out. Learn to listen a lot. You can learn a lot by listening. God ordained the older women to teach the younger women.

"Older women likewise are to be… teaching what is good, so that they may encourage the young women to love their husbands, to love their children, to be sensible, pure, workers at home, kind, being subject to their own husbands, so that the word of God will not be dishonored" (Titus 2:3-5).

HONOR YOUR PARENTS

Your days will be long if you honor your parents. Treat your parents always with great respect. Show love that is unconditional. They already love you unconditionally. Find time to spend with your mom and dad. They will always be a part of your life. They will always be a support system for you. Trust your parents. They are there to guide you even if you are twenty-one.

MENSTRUAL CYCLE

Mothers should provide their daughters with much information before she begins her cycle. A mother should be the one to train the daughter on how to care for herself during that time. Young women are starting their cycle much sooner now than when we were teenagers. Some will start as early as ten. Both mother and daughter should be ready. Talk to your daughter and tell her about what is going to happen. Use mother whit to explain this new experience. Show the daughter how to use a pad. Give her the pros and cons on using tampons or pads. Discuss the importance of being sanitary and keeping the body clean and fresh. When her underwear gets soiled, show her how to get rid of blood stains by using a laundry stain remover. Teach her the importance of discarding dirty pads by wrapping them in tissue paper and placing it in a plastic bag for the trash can. Do not leave dirty pads in the trash in the bedroom, bathroom, or under the bed. The training given to girls at school on this matter is nothing compared to what a loving, warm, and sensitive mother can give to her daughter. The following website is good for explaining the symptoms of the menstrual cycle. http://www.always.com/en-us/life-stage/teens/pad/first-periods/first-period-signs.aspx .

DATING

Do not start dating because your friends are dating. Follow your parent's rules. They know if you are mature enough to date. Dating at age thirteen is too young. Start with friendships without kissing and touching. Friendships can develop into a more intimate relationship. My recommendation is to wait until you are eighteen. Now you are in college where friendships develop into lifetime relationships. Is this the right time to date? Certainly, you still need to be mature enough to date. Do not allow yourself to be an experiment to some young man. You are very special to God. He intended that you save your virginity until you are married.

Parents should be opened minded to whom the daughter is dating. As a parent, you have already instructed her not to date someone riding a bicycle or wearing baggy pants. Young women should demand respect for themselves. Allow the young man to open the door of the car or entrance into a doorway. Do not allow a man to be touching all over your body and kissing your lips. This could be dangerous and lead to something else.

Dating is a step down from marriage. Watch and pray! Observe his character. Watch for a holy lifestyle. Watch to see if his words match his character. Listen to his words and expressions. Dress code is also important! If he wears his pants down low, then this is not the one for you. Remember now, you can't change anyone; Jesus has to change his heart and his way of thinking about himself. Watch and listen to see if he has a plan for his life, like you do. If he does not have a plan, he is not for you. He should have a plan that incorporates education, career, investments, and etc., even where he lives are all a part of the plan. Having good credit is important for buying a vehicle. Observe how he prioritizes his affairs, even down to shopping for cloths and buying electronics.

Group dating is wise. Remember, stay focused. You want a godly man for a husband who believes and loves God with his whole being the way you do. You should be selective about who your friends are. Do not hide your relationship with Christ. Pray over your food even in public. Your true friends will respect that. Do not try to be something or someone that you are not. Love yourself. Take care of yourself. Plan to marry. Do not rush in dating or building that relationship, however, do not date anyone for five to ten years. Date for at least six months to a year, if he is the one, he will ask to marry you. Do not pursue any man. Wait for God to send the right man to you. He should find you.

SEX

Sex is for marriage between a man and a woman. Homosexuality is a spirit that is looking for a place of residence. Mothers and fathers give godly guidance to your daughter. Use the scriptures and explain what Jesus taught to the disciples and left on record for us. He addressed singleness, marriage, and homosexuality. Do not shelter her so much that she will be ignorant to life skills. Share stories and articles with her to prompt questions.

Mothers explain to your daughter what pornography is and how to avoid the pitfalls and how it would discredit her relationship with Christ. Be honest and sincere with her.

MARRIAGE

Daughters' if you desire a husband, ask the Lord for a Godly husband. Mothers' encourage your daughter to pray, pray, and pray until Jesus releases a husband for you. Build a relationship as a friend to the man. Do not become eager to date anyone. Through friendship you can learn a lot about a person. Do not be eager for marriage.

Encourage your daughter to live for Christ. Daughters should be happy to be a virgin. Mothers and fathers should be an example of Christian living and a life of holiness. Parents should be open-minded about inter-racial marriage. Discuss the pros and cons of inter-racial marriage with your daughters or sons.

KEEP YOUR HOME CLEAN

God will give you your heart desire. If you chose to live in an apartment, condo, or a house, keep it clean. Do not allow your home to become rat and roach infested.

CLEANING UP

When working in the kitchen, always start with fresh hot dishwater and soap. Clean up as you go, and you will not invite roaches, mice, or other rodents into your home. Keep the trash bins emptied. Wipe down you stove, refrigerator, and counter tops to keep down germs. Be careful with bleach. The odor is very strong and dangerous. Use gloves when doing household chores and cleaning with chemicals. Do not fail to dust and take care of your furniture. Use broom to swish the corners of walls and ceilings to keep down cob webs. Make sure to dusk around ceiling fans.

BE ACTIVE

Being active comes with being fit for health sake. Exercise daily is important along with a good diet. Years to come will prove being healthy and active is worthwhile. Join a gym! Get your exercise in every day. Walk a mile or two with someone. It will keep your sugar low and burn up calories.

COMMON SENSE

What is common sense?

Common sense is, according to Merriam Dictionary, the ability to think and behave in a reasonable way and to make good decisions.

Use common sense! Using common sense does not require a college degree to make a common sense decision. Be alert! Be vigilant! Use wisdom in making decisions. A wrong decision will cost you to suffer the consequences, sometimes, for the rest of your life. Learn to think through the decision process. Do not be sloppy in your thought processes. You will be glad that you thought it through.

SKIN, HAIR, & NAIL CARE

Begin to care for your skin early. Perhaps I should remind you of how your mother nurtured your skin as a child. You were trained to oil down daily. Here is a history note! As a child, my mother used lard that came from a pig on us daily to oil our skin. We could not aford the costly products of lotion or hair grease. Later in life, my mother introduced us to Vaseline and Royal Crown hairdresser. We were taught to use Noxema for the face and Ponds facial cream. We had no training on how to care for the skin. Now there are many products on the market for skin care. Know your own skin and proceed to use what is best for your skin. Make sure you eat properly to get the nutrients for skin, hair, and nail care. Learn to care properly for you. Do not start using the cosmopolitan nails; constant use will damage your nail bed and stunt the natural growth. Know your own hair.

After seeing a dermatologist, I learned that perms are not for everyone. As a personal testimony, I lost a lot of hair. It simply thinned out, especially in the top of my scalp. I found out late in life that my hair was damaged due to perms and constant heat. The beautician will not tell you this until after the fact. Do your own research.

One other note concerning your skin, make sure the deodorant you use is aluminum free. It has been studied and documented that aluminum is in your antiperspirant deodorants and the studies show it is a high risk to use them. I have found that aluminum free deodorants are just as effective as antiperspirants. If you use the antiperspirant deodorants, clean under the arm pit and around the neck and behind the ears weekly. Here are a view websites that will help you in your research.

1. http://www.webmd.com/skin-problems-and-treatments/features/antiperspirant-facts-safety
2. http://www.collective-evolution.com/2013/09/14/attention-deodorant-users-new-studies-link-aluminum-to-breast-cancer/
3. http://www.ncbi.nlm.nih.gov/pubmed/16045991

MOTHER DAUGHTER TIPS BY OTHER MOTHERS

Submitted by My Sister: Reverend Pinkie Hill

My daughter Yvonne has always been very independent. I recognized that as a strength and encouraged that quality in her life. I gave her room to choose her clothes, her hair style, her friends and most times, we ended up in agreement. Shoe shopping was an event which we didn't always agree, but one thing she looked for was comfort. I remember her senior year in high school, she was determined to become president of student counsel, and she ran and won even thou the odds were against her. At the end of the year she decided she was going into the Army. Other students were planning for college, but not Yvonne. It was not until the signing of the contract did she break down crying and called home telling me that she changed her mind, "I do not want to go". I was so relieved, but I allowed that decision to be hers. Even today as an adult, her decisions are hers. I just pray.

WHAT I SAID TO MY DAUGHTER

By Pastor Dr. Wilma J. Brown-Foreman, Ed. S

Mother Teresa profoundly said: "Love has no other message but its own. Every day we try to live out Christ's love in a very tangible way in every one of our deeds. If we do any preaching, it is done with deeds, not with words."[1]

My daughter lost her father when she was in the second grade. At the age of forty, I was left as a widow to rear a thirteen year old son just entering high school and my six year old daughter. Needless to say, this stage of life was not easy.

I am the type of mother that believes in showing my children how much I love them-not always by words, but by my actions.

---

[1] Gonzalez-balado, Mother Teresa, Loving Jesus, (Arbor, Michigan: Servant Publications, 1991)

Through my efforts to provide for them, my deeds spoke for me. Throughout the difficult years of being both a mother and father, I had to depend on God for wisdom, provisions, perseverance, and faith in His ability to sustain us from day to day, week to week, and year to year.

All mothers will find that times will come for "tough love." These were the times when I had to temper the strong will of my daughter when I saw her heading down the wrong paths in life. To say "No!" to her was much more of a challenge than it was to say that word to my son.

To tell her to choose her friends more wisely was another hard, but very needful assignment as a mother. To point her to a Christian college after she graduated from high school was one of my greatest challenges, since she insisted on attending colleges with some of her favorite high school buddies. In any case, I found that even when I was hurting inside because our minds and spirits clashed, I still had to show her how much I loved her by prayerfully helping to direct her decisions and courses of actions that I believed were best for her in the eyes and plans of God. As all of us can attest, sometimes, I failed.

I learned that more than anything, I had to find the strength to tell and show my daughter that I could still love her when she faltered in life. After the motherly reprimands, chides, and threats, came forgiveness and reconciliation. I always want my daughter to know that I love her-even when she does not live up to my expectations, as God loves us when we fail Him. Romans 5:8 tells us: "But God commendeth his love toward us, in that, while we were yet sinners, Christ died for us."

He *demonstrated* how much He loved us without saying a word. Our deeds speak for us in our daily walks with our children. Praying for them, keeping them in church, offering godly counsel, and teaching them to trust God through every situation are all invaluable lessons, however, they are better lived out than always verbally expressed. What I have said to my daughter has been expressed in my actions toward her each day.

It was a joy in writing this book. To every reader, thank you for

reading my book.

Dr. Sharon E. Peterson

Printed in the United States
By Bookmasters